Note from the author

Thank you for purchasing Explore Utah! This coloring book is designed to be as fun as it is educational. We hope to excite and engage you with some of Utah's most notable and celebrated places within these active pages and diverse scenes.

This book has been designed with the help of my illustrator, Gabriele Liedtke, and countless educators, parents, friends, and of course, children. We have incorporated your feedback and crafted this book to inspire conversations about those places in Utah that many of us hold as special in both our hearts and minds.

Thank you for helping us visualize part of Utah in these pages. We are excited to see you make the immense natural and physical scenery of Utah come alive.

Best regards,

Ben Brinkopf
Ben@ColoringtoLearn.com

About Coloring to Learn
Coloring to Learn, LLC is a children's coloring book producer that celebrates unique and unforgettable sights and attractions. Specializing in fun and educational drawings for young children, we believe that coloring books deserve a prominent place in a child's life. Children crave mental engagement and physical activity to broaden their talents and develop critical thinking skills. In a world dominated by more technology and entertainment than ever, coloring books have attained an even more important role in ensuring our children get the stimulation they need to learn and grow.

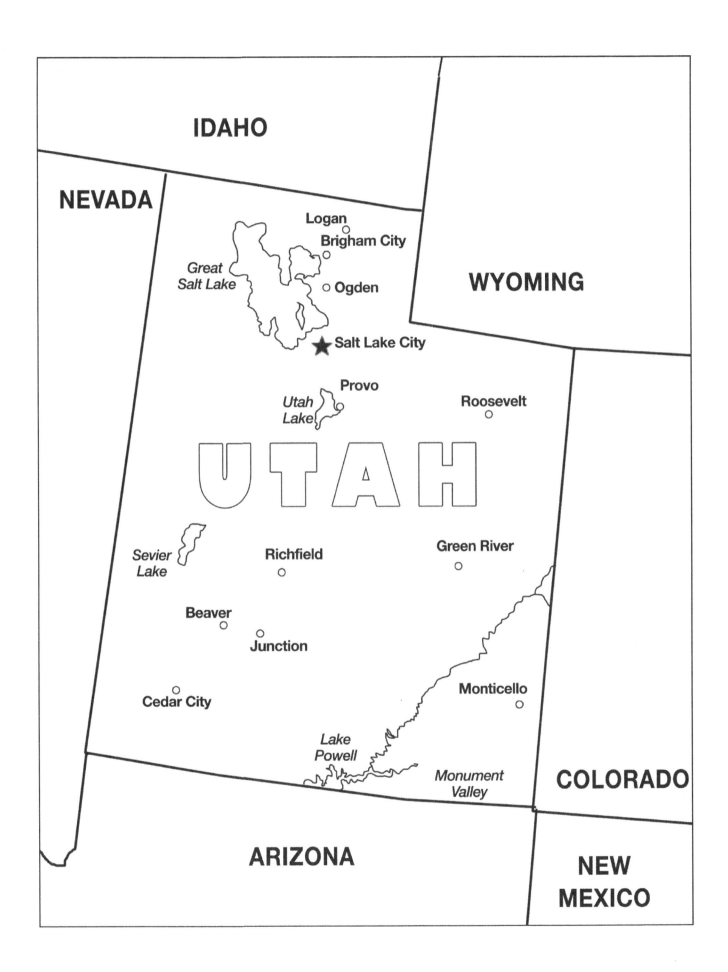

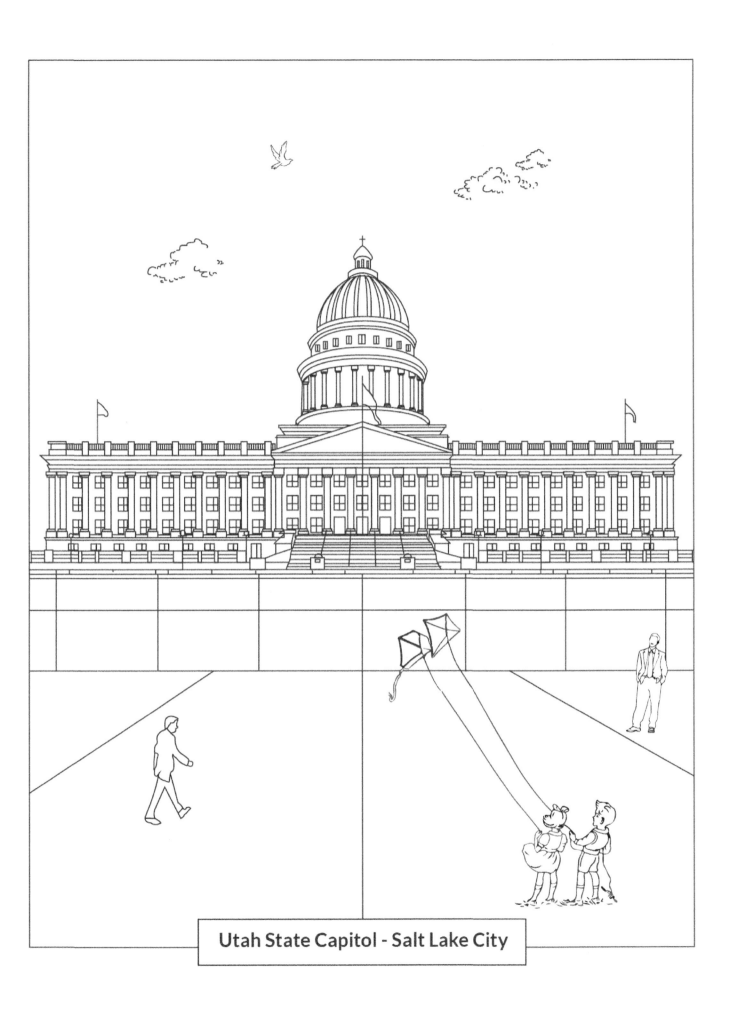

This is the Place Monument

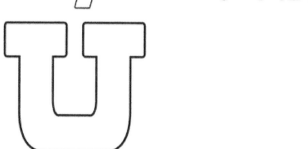

Made in the USA
Las Vegas, NV
13 July 2024